MznLnx

Missing Links Exam Preps

Exam Prep for

Beginning and Intermediate Algebra

Miller, O'Neill, & Hyde, 2nd Edition

The MznLnx Exam Prep is your link from the texbook and lecture to your exams.
The MznLnx Exam Preps are unauthorized and comprehensive reviews of your textbooks.

All material provided by MznLnx and Rico Publications (c) 2010
Textbook publishers and textbook authors do not particpate in or contribute to these reviews.

MznLnx

Rico Publications

Exam Prep for Beginning and Intermediate Algebra
2nd Edition
Miller, O'Neill, & Hyde

Publisher: Raymond Houge
Assistant Editor: Michael Rouger
Text and Cover Designer: Lisa Buckner
Marketing Manager: Sara Swagger
Project Manager, Editorial Production: Jerry Emerson
Art Director: Vernon Lowerui

Product Manager: Dave Mason
Editorial Assitant: Rachel Guzmanji
Pedagogy: Debra Long
Cover Image: Jim Reed/Getty Images
Text and Cover Printer: City Printing, Inc.
Compositor: Media Mix, Inc.

(c) 2010 Rico Publications

ALL RIGHTS RESERVED. No part of this work covered by the copyright may be reproduced or used in any form or by an means--graphic, electronic, or mechanical, including photocopying, recording, taping, Web distribution, information storage, and retrieval systems, or in any other manner--without the written permission of the publisher.

For more information about our products, contact us at:
Dave.Mason@RicoPublications.com

For permission to use material from this text or product, submit a request online to:
Dave.Mason@RicoPublications.com

Printed in the United States
ISBN:

Contents

CHAPTER 1
The Set of Real Numbers — 1

CHAPTER 2
Linear Equations and Inequalities — 8

CHAPTER 3
Graphing Linear Equations in Two Variables — 11

CHAPTER 4
Systems of Linear Equations in Two Variables — 14

CHAPTER 5
Polynomials and Properties of Exponents — 15

CHAPTER 6
Factoring Polynomials — 18

CHAPTER 7
Rational Expressions — 22

CHAPTER 8
Introduction to Relations and Functions — 24

CHAPTER 9
Systems of Linear Equations in Three Variables — 27

CHAPTER 10
More Equations and Inequalities — 30

CHAPTER 11
Radicals and Complex Numbers — 32

CHAPTER 12
Quadratic Equations and Functions — 36

CHAPTER 13
Exponential and Logarithmic Functions — 39

CHAPTER 14
Conic Sections and Nonlinear Systems — 43

ANSWER KEY — 46

TO THE STUDENT

COMPREHENSIVE

The *MznLnx* Exam Prep series is designed to help you pass your exams. Editors at MznLnx review your textbooks and then prepare these practice exams to help you master the textbook material. Unlike study guides, workbooks, and practice tests provided by the texbook publisher and textbook authors, *MznLnx* gives you **all** of the material in each chapter in exam form, not just samples, so you can be sure to nail your exam.

MECHANICAL

The MznLnx Exam Prep series creates exams that will help you learn the subject matter as well as test you on your understanding. Each question is designed to help you master the concept. Just working through the exams, you gain an understanding of the subject--its a simple mechanical process that produces success.

INTEGRATED STUDY GUIDE AND REVIEW

MznLnx is not just a set of exams designed to test you, its also a comprehensive review of the subject content. Each exam question is also a review of the concept, making sure that you will get the answer correct without having to go to other sources of material. You learn as you go! Its the easiest way to pass an exam.

HUMOR

Studying can be tedious and dry. MznLnx's instructional design includes moderate humor within the exam questions on occassion, to break the tedium and revitalize the brain

Chapter 1. The Set of Real Numbers

1. The mathematical concept of a _____ expresses the intuitive idea of deterministic dependence between two quantities, one of which is viewed as primary and the other as secondary. A _____ then is a way to associate a unique output for each input of a specified type, for example, a real number or an element of a given set.
    a. Thing
    b. Function1
    c. Undefined
    d. Undefined

2. In mathematics, a _____ may be described informally as a number that can be given by an infinite decimal representation.
    a. Thing
    b. Real number2
    c. Undefined
    d. Undefined

3. An _____ is a mathematical statement, in symbols, that two things are the same or equivalent. Equations are written with an equal sign, as in 2 + 3 = 5.
    a. Equation3
    b. Thing
    c. Undefined
    d. Undefined

4. In mathematics, a _____ is a number in the form of a + bi where a and b are real numbers, and i is the imaginary unit, with the property i 2 = −1. The real number a is called the real part of the _____, and the real number b is the imaginary part.
    a. Thing
    b. Complex number4
    c. Undefined
    d. Undefined

5. In mathematics, _____ is the decomposition of an object into a product of other objects, or factors, which when multiplied together give the original.
    a. Thing
    b. Factoring5
    c. Undefined
    d. Undefined

6. _____, in number theory is the process of breaking down a composite number into smaller non-trivial divisors, which when multiplied together equal the original integer.
   a. Integer factorization6
   b. Thing
   c. Undefined
   d. Undefined

7. _____ is the mathematical operation of combining or adding two numbers to obtain an equal simple amount or total.
   a. Addition7
   b. Thing
   c. Undefined
   d. Undefined

8. _____ is the distance around a given two-dimensional object. As a general rule, the _____ of a polygon can always be calculated by adding all the length of the sides together. So, the formula for triangles is P = a + b + c, where a, b and c stand for each side of it. For quadrilaterals the equation is P = a + b + c + d. For equilateral polygons, P = na, where n is the number of sides and a is the side length.
   a. Thing
   b. Perimeter8
   c. Undefined
   d. Undefined

9. In Euclidean geometry, a _____ is the set of all points in a plane at a fixed distance, called the radius, from a given point, the center.
   a. Circle9
   b. Thing
   c. Undefined
   d. Undefined

10. In geometry, a _____ is defined as a quadrilateral where all four of its angles are right angles.
    a. Rectangle10
    b. Thing
    c. Undefined
    d. Undefined

Chapter 1. The Set of Real Numbers 3

11. In plane geometry, a _____ is a polygon with four equal sides, four right angles, and parallel opposite sides. In algebra, the _____ of a number is that number multiplied by itself.
   a. Square11
   b. Thing
   c. Undefined
   d. Undefined

12. In mathematics, a _____ is a quadric surface, with the following equation in Cartesian coordinates: $(x/_a)^2 + (y/_b)^2 = 1$.
   a. Thing
   b. Cylinder12
   c. Undefined
   d. Undefined

13. In mathematics, a _____ is the set of all points in three-dimensional space (R^3) which are at distance r from a fixed point of that space, where r is a positive real number called the radius of the _____. The fixed point is called the center or centre, and is not part of the _____ itself.
   a. Sphere13
   b. Thing
   c. Undefined
   d. Undefined

14. The _____ of a solid object is the three-dimensional concept of how much space it occupies, often quantified numerically.
   a. Thing
   b. Volume14
   c. Undefined
   d. Undefined

15. An angle smaller than a right angle is called an _____ (less than 90 degrees).
   a. Thing
   b. Acute angle15
   c. Undefined
   d. Undefined

16. In a function the _____, is the variable which is the value, i.e. the "output", of the function.

a. Dependent variable16
b. Thing
c. Undefined
d. Undefined

17. In mathematics, the _____ of two sets A and B is the set that contains all elements of A that also belong to B (or equivalently, all elements of B that also belong to A), but no other elements.
a. Thing
b. Intersection17
c. Undefined
d. Undefined

18. The existence and properties of _____ are the basis of Euclid's parallel postulate. _____ are two lines on the same plane that do not intersect even assuming that lines extend to infinity in either direction.
a. Parallel lines18
b. Thing
c. Undefined
d. Undefined

19. In geometry and trigonometry, a _____ is defined as an angle between two straight intersecting lines of ninety degrees, or one-quarter of a circle.
a. Right angle19
b. Thing
c. Undefined
d. Undefined

20. An angle equal to two right angles is called a _____ (equal to 180 degrees).
a. Thing
b. Straight angle20
c. Undefined
d. Undefined

21. A pair of angles are said to be _____ if they share the same vertex and are bounded by the same pair of lines but are opposite to each other. They are also congruent.

a. Thing
b. Vertical angles21
c. Undefined
d. Undefined

22. A _____ is a symbolic representation denoting a quantity or expression. It often represents an "unknown" quantity that has the potential to change.
   a. Thing
   b. Variable22
   c. Undefined
   d. Undefined

23. An _____ is a triangle that has one internal angle larger than 90°
   a. Obtuse triangle23
   b. Thing
   c. Undefined
   d. Undefined

24. In mathematics, the _____ of a number n is the number that, when added to n, yields zero. The _____ of n is denoted −n. For example, 7 is −7, because 7 + (−7) = 0, and the _____ of −0.3 is 0.3, because −0.3 + 0.3 = 0.
   a. Additive inverse24
   b. Thing
   c. Undefined
   d. Undefined

25. Mathematical _____ is used in mathematics, and throughout the physical sciences, engineering, and economics. The complexity of such _____ ranges from relatively simple symbolic representations, such as numbers 1 and 2; function symbols sin and +, to conceptual symbols, such as lim and dy/dx; to equations and variables.
   a. Thing
   b. Notation25
   c. Undefined
   d. Undefined

26. _____ usually occurs when an exact form or an exact numerical number is unknown.

Chapter 1. The Set of Real Numbers

a. Thing
b. Approximation26
c. Undefined
d. Undefined

27. An _____ is a combination of numbers, operators, grouping symbols and/or free variables and bound variables arranged in a meaningful way which can be evaluated..
   a. Thing
   b. Expression27
   c. Undefined
   d. Undefined

28. In mathematics, a _____ is the end result of a division problem. It can also be expressed as the number of times the divisor divides into the dividend.
   a. Quotient28
   b. Thing
   c. Undefined
   d. Undefined

29. _____ is a mathematical operation, written a^n, involving two numbers, the base a and the exponent n.
   a. Thing
   b. Exponentiating29
   c. Undefined
   d. Undefined

30. In mathematics, a _____ of a complex-valued function f is a member x of the domain of f such that f(x) vanishes at x, that is, x : f (x) = 0.
   a. Thing
   b. Root30
   c. Undefined
   d. Undefined

31. In mathematics, a _____ of a number x is a number r such that $r^2 = x$, or in words, a number r whose square (the result of multiplying the number by itself) is x.

Chapter 1. The Set of Real Numbers

a. Square root31
b. Thing
c. Undefined
d. Undefined

32. In philosophy, mathematics, and logic, a _____ is an attribute of an object; thus a red object is said to have the _____ of redness.
   a. Thing
   b. Property32
   c. Undefined
   d. Undefined

33. In mathematics, _____ is a property that a binary operation can have. Within an expression containing two or more of the same associative operators in a row, the order of operations does not matter as long as the sequence of the operands is not changed.
   a. Associativity33
   b. Thing
   c. Undefined
   d. Undefined

34. An _____ is an equality that remains true regardless of the values of any variables that appear within it, to distinguish it from an equality which is true under more particular conditions.
   a. Identity34
   b. Thing
   c. Undefined
   d. Undefined

35. The word _____ comes from the Latin word linearis, which means created by lines.
   a. Thing
   b. Linear35
   c. Undefined
   d. Undefined

Chapter 2. Linear Equations and Inequalities

1. An _____ is a mathematical statement, in symbols, that two things are the same or equivalent. Equations are written with an equal sign, as in 2 + 3 = 5.
   a. Thing
   b. Equation1
   c. Undefined
   d. Undefined

2. _____ is the mathematical operation of combining or adding two numbers to obtain an equal simple amount or total.
   a. Addition2
   b. Thing
   c. Undefined
   d. Undefined

3. In philosophy, mathematics, and logic, a _____ is an attribute of an object; thus a red object is said to have the _____ of redness.
   a. Property3
   b. Thing
   c. Undefined
   d. Undefined

4. The word _____ comes from the Latin word linearis, which means created by lines.
   a. Linear4
   b. Thing
   c. Undefined
   d. Undefined

5. A _____ is a symbolic representation denoting a quantity or expression. It often represents an "unknown" quantity that has the potential to change.
   a. Variable5
   b. Thing
   c. Undefined
   d. Undefined

Chapter 2. Linear Equations and Inequalities

6. _____ is the distance around a given two-dimensional object. As a general rule, the _____ of a polygon can always be calculated by adding all the length of the sides together. So, the formula for triangles is P = a + b + c, where a, b and c stand for each side of it. For quadrilaterals the equation is P = a + b + c + d. For equilateral polygons, P = na, where n is the number of sides and a is the side length.
   a. Thing
   b. Perimeter6
   c. Undefined
   d. Undefined

7. A pair of angles are _____ if the sum of their angles is 90°.
   a. Thing
   b. Complementary7
   c. Undefined
   d. Undefined

8. In geometry, a _____ is defined as a quadrilateral where all four of its angles are right angles.
   a. Thing
   b. Rectangle8
   c. Undefined
   d. Undefined

9. In mathematics, a _____ is an expression that is constructed from one or more variables and constants, using only the operations of addition, subtraction, multiplication, and constant positive whole number exponents. is a _____. Note in particular that division by an expression containing a variable is not in general allowed in polynomials.
   a. Polynomial9
   b. Thing
   c. Undefined
   d. Undefined

10. An _____ is a function which does the reverse of a given function.
    a. Inverse function10
    b. Thing
    c. Undefined
    d. Undefined

11. In Euclidean geometry, a _____ is the set of all points in a plane at a fixed distance, called the radius, from a given point, the center.
   a. Circle11
   b. Thing
   c. Undefined
   d. Undefined

12. The mathematical concept of a _____ expresses the intuitive idea of deterministic dependence between two quantities, one of which is viewed as primary and the other as secondary. A _____ then is a way to associate a unique output for each input of a specified type, for example, a real number or an element of a given set.
   a. Function12
   b. Thing
   c. Undefined
   d. Undefined

13. In elementary algebra, an _____ is a set that contains every real number between two indicated numbers and may contain the two numbers themselves.
   a. Interval13
   b. Thing
   c. Undefined
   d. Undefined

14. _____ is the notation in which permitted values for a variable are expressed as ranging over a certain interval; "5 < x < 9" is an example of the application of _____.
   a. Interval notation14
   b. Thing
   c. Undefined
   d. Undefined

15. Mathematical _____ is used in mathematics, and throughout the physical sciences, engineering, and economics. The complexity of such _____ ranges from relatively simple symbolic representations, such as numbers 1 and 2; function symbols sin and +, to conceptual symbols, such as lim and dy/dx; to equations and variables.
   a. Thing
   b. Notation15
   c. Undefined
   d. Undefined

Chapter 3. Graphing Linear Equations in Two Variables

1. An _____ is a mathematical statement, in symbols, that two things are the same or equivalent. Equations are written with an equal sign, as in 2 + 3 = 5.
   a. Thing
   b. Equation1
   c. Undefined
   d. Undefined

2. The word _____ comes from the Latin word linearis, which means created by lines.
   a. Linear2
   b. Thing
   c. Undefined
   d. Undefined

3. A _____ is a symbolic representation denoting a quantity or expression. It often represents an "unknown" quantity that has the potential to change.
   a. Thing
   b. Variable3
   c. Undefined
   d. Undefined

4. In astronomy, geography, geometry and related sciences and contexts, a plane is said to be _____ at a given point if it is locally perpendicular to the gradient of the gravity field, i.e., with the direction of the gravitational force at that point.
   a. Horizontal4
   b. Thing
   c. Undefined
   d. Undefined

5. _____ is often used to describe the measurement of the steepness, incline, gradient, or grade of a straight line. The _____ is defined as the ratio of the "rise" divided by the "run" between two points on a line, or in other words, the ratio of the altitude change to the horizontal distance between any two points on the line.
   a. Thing
   b. Slope5
   c. Undefined
   d. Undefined

6. In mathematics, the _____ of a function is the set of all "output" values produced by that function. Given a function $f : A \to B$, the _____ of f, is defined to be the set $\{x \in B : x = f(a) \text{ for some } a \in A\}$.

Chapter 3. Graphing Linear Equations in Two Variables

   a. Thing
   b. Range6
   c. Undefined
   d. Undefined

7. The existence and properties of _____ are the basis of Euclid's parallel postulate. _____ are two lines on the same plane that do not intersect even assuming that lines extend to infinity in either direction.
   a. Thing
   b. Parallel lines7
   c. Undefined
   d. Undefined

8. _____ is a notation for writing numbers that is often used by scientists and mathematicians to make it easier to write large and small numbers.
   a. Scientific notation8
   b. Thing
   c. Undefined
   d. Undefined

9. In plane geometry, a _____ is a polygon with four equal sides, four right angles, and parallel opposite sides. In algebra, the _____ of a number is that number multiplied by itself.
   a. Square9
   b. Thing
   c. Undefined
   d. Undefined

10. In a function the _____, is the variable which is the value, i.e. the "output", of the function.
    a. Dependent variable10
    b. Thing
    c. Undefined
    d. Undefined

11. In mathematics, an _____ is any of the arguments, i.e. "inputs", to a function. Thus if we have a function f(x), then x is a _____.

a. Independent variable11
b. Thing
c. Undefined
d. Undefined

Chapter 4. Systems of Linear Equations in Two Variables

1. An _____ is a mathematical statement, in symbols, that two things are the same or equivalent. Equations are written with an equal sign, as in 2 + 3 = 5.
   a. Equation1
   b. Thing
   c. Undefined
   d. Undefined

2. The word _____ comes from the Latin word linearis, which means created by lines.
   a. Thing
   b. Linear2
   c. Undefined
   d. Undefined

3. A _____ is a symbolic representation denoting a quantity or expression. It often represents an "unknown" quantity that has the potential to change.
   a. Variable3
   b. Thing
   c. Undefined
   d. Undefined

4. _____ is the mathematical operation of combining or adding two numbers to obtain an equal simple amount or total.
   a. Thing
   b. Addition4
   c. Undefined
   d. Undefined

Chapter 5. Polynomials and Properties of Exponents

1. _____ is a mathematical operation, written a^n, involving two numbers, the base a and the exponent n.
   a. Thing
   b. Exponentiating1
   c. Undefined
   d. Undefined

2. Mathematical _____ is used in mathematics, and throughout the physical sciences, engineering, and economics. The complexity of such _____ ranges from relatively simple symbolic representations, such as numbers 1 and 2; function symbols sin and +, to conceptual symbols, such as lim and dy/dx; to equations and variables.
   a. Notation2
   b. Thing
   c. Undefined
   d. Undefined

3. The _____ governs the differentiation of products of differentiable functions.
   a. Thing
   b. Product rule3
   c. Undefined
   d. Undefined

4. In mathematics, a _____ is the end result of a division problem. It can also be expressed as the number of times the divisor divides into the dividend.
   a. Quotient4
   b. Thing
   c. Undefined
   d. Undefined

5. A _____ is a special kind of ratio, indicating a relationship between two measurements with different units, such as miles to gallons or cents to pounds.
   a. Thing
   b. Rate5
   c. Undefined
   d. Undefined

6. In mathematics, a _____ is an expression that is constructed from one or more variables and constants, using only the operations of addition, subtraction, multiplication, and constant positive whole number exponents. is a _____. Note in particular that division by an expression containing a variable is not in general allowed in polynomials.

Chapter 5. Polynomials and Properties of Exponents

    a. Polynomial6
    b. Thing
    c. Undefined
    d. Undefined

7. A _____ is a symbolic representation denoting a quantity or expression. It often represents an "unknown" quantity that has the potential to change.
    a. Variable7
    b. Thing
    c. Undefined
    d. Undefined

8. _____ is the mathematical operation of combining or adding two numbers to obtain an equal simple amount or total.
    a. Thing
    b. Addition8
    c. Undefined
    d. Undefined

9. The _____ is commonly taught to US high school students learning algebra as a mnemonic for remembering how to multiply two binomials.
    a. Thing
    b. FOIL rule9
    c. Undefined
    d. Undefined

10. In Euclidean geometry, a _____ is the set of all points in a plane at a fixed distance, called the radius, from a given point, the center.
    a. Circle10
    b. Thing
    c. Undefined
    d. Undefined

11. In mathematics, the _____ is a conic section generated by the intersection of a right circular conical surface and a plane parallel to a generating straight line of that surface. It can also be defined as locus of points in a plane which are equidistant from a given point.

a. Thing
b. Parabola11
c. Undefined
d. Undefined

12. In plane geometry, a _____ is a polygon with four equal sides, four right angles, and parallel opposite sides. In algebra, the _____ of a number is that number multiplied by itself.
a. Thing
b. Square12
c. Undefined
d. Undefined

Chapter 6. Factoring Polynomials

1. In mathematics, an _____ is any of the arguments, i.e. "inputs", to a function. Thus if we have a function f(x), then x is a _____.
   a. Independent variable1
   b. Thing
   c. Undefined
   d. Undefined

2. _____, in number theory is the process of breaking down a composite number into smaller non-trivial divisors, which when multiplied together equal the original integer.
   a. Thing
   b. Integer factorization2
   c. Undefined
   d. Undefined

3. In mathematics, a _____ is an expression that is constructed from one or more variables and constants, using only the operations of addition, subtraction, multiplication, and constant positive whole number exponents. is a _____. Note in particular that division by an expression containing a variable is not in general allowed in polynomials.
   a. Polynomial3
   b. Thing
   c. Undefined
   d. Undefined

4. A _____ is a symbolic representation denoting a quantity or expression. It often represents an "unknown" quantity that has the potential to change.
   a. Variable4
   b. Thing
   c. Undefined
   d. Undefined

5. An _____ is a combination of numbers, operators, grouping symbols and/or free variables and bound variables arranged in a meaningful way which can be evaluated..
   a. Expression5
   b. Thing
   c. Undefined
   d. Undefined

Chapter 6. Factoring Polynomials

6. In plane geometry, a _____ is a polygon with four equal sides, four right angles, and parallel opposite sides. In algebra, the _____ of a number is that number multiplied by itself.
   a. Square6
   b. Thing
   c. Undefined
   d. Undefined

7. _____ is the mathematical operation of combining or adding two numbers to obtain an equal simple amount or total.
   a. Addition7
   b. Thing
   c. Undefined
   d. Undefined

8. An _____ is a mathematical statement, in symbols, that two things are the same or equivalent. Equations are written with an equal sign, as in 2 + 3 = 5.
   a. Thing
   b. Equation8
   c. Undefined
   d. Undefined

9. The _____ governs the differentiation of products of differentiable functions.
   a. Thing
   b. Product rule9
   c. Undefined
   d. Undefined

10. In mathematics, a _____ is a polynomial equation of the second degree. The general form is $ax^2 + bx + c = 0$.
    a. Quadratic equation10
    b. Thing
    c. Undefined
    d. Undefined

11. The word _____ comes from the Latin word linearis, which means created by lines.

a. Thing
b. Linear11
c. Undefined
d. Undefined

12. In mathematics, a _____ is a statement that can be proved on the basis of explicitly stated or previously agreed assumptions.
    a. Theorem12
    b. Thing
    c. Undefined
    d. Undefined

13. In mathematics, a _____ of a k-place relation $L \subseteq X_1 \times ... \times X_k$ is one of the sets X_j, $1 \leq j \leq k$. In the special case where k = 2 and $L \subseteq X_1 \times X_2$ is a function $L : X_1 \to X_2$, it is conventional to refer to X_1 as the _____ of the function and to refer to X_2 as the codomain of the function.
    a. Thing
    b. Domain13
    c. Undefined
    d. Undefined

14. The mathematical concept of a _____ expresses the intuitive idea of deterministic dependence between two quantities, one of which is viewed as primary and the other as secondary. A _____ then is a way to associate a unique output for each input of a specified type, for example, a real number or an element of a given set.
    a. Function14
    b. Thing
    c. Undefined
    d. Undefined

15. In set theory and other branches of mathematics, the _____ of a collection of sets is the set that contains everything that belongs to any of the sets, but nothing else.
    a. Thing
    b. Union15
    c. Undefined
    d. Undefined

16. A _____ is a special kind of ratio, indicating a relationship between two measurements with different units, such as miles to gallons or cents to pounds.
   a. Thing
   b. Rate16
   c. Undefined
   d. Undefined

Chapter 7. Rational Expressions

1. In mathematics, a _____ of a k-place relation $L \subseteq X_1 \times \ldots \times X_k$ is one of the sets X_j, $1 \leq j \leq k$. In the special case where k = 2 and $L \subseteq X_1 \times X_2$ is a function $L : X_1 \to X_2$, it is conventional to refer to X_1 as the _____ of the function and to refer to X_2 as the codomain of the function.
   a. Domain1
   b. Thing
   c. Undefined
   d. Undefined

2. The mathematical concept of a _____ expresses the intuitive idea of deterministic dependence between two quantities, one of which is viewed as primary and the other as secondary. A _____ then is a way to associate a unique output for each input of a specified type, for example, a real number or an element of a given set.
   a. Thing
   b. Function2
   c. Undefined
   d. Undefined

3. _____ is the mathematical operation of combining or adding two numbers to obtain an equal simple amount or total.
   a. Addition3
   b. Thing
   c. Undefined
   d. Undefined

4. An _____ is a mathematical statement, in symbols, that two things are the same or equivalent. Equations are written with an equal sign, as in 2 + 3 = 5.
   a. Equation4
   b. Thing
   c. Undefined
   d. Undefined

5. The word _____ comes from the Latin word linearis, which means created by lines.
   a. Thing
   b. Linear5
   c. Undefined
   d. Undefined

Chapter 7. Rational Expressions 23

6. A _____ is a symbolic representation denoting a quantity or expression. It often represents an "unknown" quantity that has the potential to change.
   a. Thing
   b. Variable6
   c. Undefined
   d. Undefined

7. _____ is a mathematical operation, written a^n, involving two numbers, the base a and the exponent n.
   a. Exponentiating7
   b. Thing
   c. Undefined
   d. Undefined

8. A quadratic equation with real solutions, called roots, which may be real or complex, is given by the _____: $x = \frac{-b \pm \sqrt{b^2 - 4ac}}{2a}$.
   a. Quadratic formula8
   b. Thing
   c. Undefined
   d. Undefined

9. _____ is a special mathematical relationship between two quantities. Two quantities are called proportional if they vary in such a way that one of the quantities is a constant multiple of the other, or equivalently if they have a constant ratio.
   a. Thing
   b. Proportionality9
   c. Undefined
   d. Undefined

10. A _____ is a special kind of ratio, indicating a relationship between two measurements with different units, such as miles to gallons or cents to pounds.
    a. Rate10
    b. Thing
    c. Undefined
    d. Undefined

Chapter 8. Introduction to Relations and Functions

1. In mathematics, a _____ of a k-place relation $L \subseteq X_1 \times ... \times X_k$ is one of the sets X_j, $1 \leq j \leq k$. In the special case where k = 2 and $L \subseteq X_1 \times X_2$ is a function $L : X_1 \rightarrow X_2$, it is conventional to refer to X_1 as the _____ of the function and to refer to X_2 as the codomain of the function.
    a. Thing
    b. Domain1
    c. Undefined
    d. Undefined

2. In mathematics, the _____ of a function is the set of all "output" values produced by that function. Given a function $f : A \rightarrow B$, the _____ of f, is defined to be the set $\{x \in B : x = f(a)$ for some $a \in A\}$.
    a. Range2
    b. Thing
    c. Undefined
    d. Undefined

3. The mathematical concept of a _____ expresses the intuitive idea of deterministic dependence between two quantities, one of which is viewed as primary and the other as secondary. A _____ then is a way to associate a unique output for each input of a specified type, for example, a real number or an element of a given set.
    a. Thing
    b. Function3
    c. Undefined
    d. Undefined

4. Mathematical _____ is used in mathematics, and throughout the physical sciences, engineering, and economics. The complexity of such _____ ranges from relatively simple symbolic representations, such as numbers 1 and 2; function symbols sin and +, to conceptual symbols, such as lim and dy/dx; to equations and variables.
    a. Thing
    b. Notation4
    c. Undefined
    d. Undefined

5. An _____ is a mathematical statement, in symbols, that two things are the same or equivalent. Equations are written with an equal sign, as in 2 + 3 = 5.
    a. Thing
    b. Equation5
    c. Undefined
    d. Undefined

Chapter 8. Introduction to Relations and Functions 25

6. The word _____ comes from the Latin word linearis, which means created by lines.
   a. Thing
   b. Linear6
   c. Undefined
   d. Undefined

7. A _____ is a symbolic representation denoting a quantity or expression. It often represents an "unknown" quantity that has the potential to change.
   a. Thing
   b. Variable7
   c. Undefined
   d. Undefined

8. _____ is a function whose values do not vary and thus are constant.
   a. Thing
   b. Constant function8
   c. Undefined
   d. Undefined

9. An _____ is a straight line or curve A to which another curve B approaches closer and closer as one moves along it. As one moves along B, the space between it and the _____ A becomes smaller and smaller, and can in fact be made as small as one could wish by going far enough along. A curve may or may not touch or cross its _____. In fact, the curve may intersect the _____ an infinite number of times.
   a. Thing
   b. Asymptote9
   c. Undefined
   d. Undefined

10. In astronomy, geography, geometry and related sciences and contexts, a plane is said to be _____ at a given point if it is locally perpendicular to the gradient of the gravity field, i.e., with the direction of the gravitational force at that point.
   a. Horizontal10
   b. Thing
   c. Undefined
   d. Undefined

11. _____ is one of the most important functions in mathematics. A function commonly used to study growth and decay
   a. Thing
   b. Exponential function11
   c. Undefined
   d. Undefined

12. In set theory and other branches of mathematics, the _____ of a collection of sets is the set that contains everything that belongs to any of the sets, but nothing else.
   a. Thing
   b. Union12
   c. Undefined
   d. Undefined

Chapter 9. Systems of Linear Equations in Three Variables

1. A _____ is a symbolic representation denoting a quantity or expression. It often represents an "unknown" quantity that has the potential to change.
   a. Variable1
   b. Thing
   c. Undefined
   d. Undefined

2. An _____ is a mathematical statement, in symbols, that two things are the same or equivalent. Equations are written with an equal sign, as in 2 + 3 = 5.
   a. Equation2
   b. Thing
   c. Undefined
   d. Undefined

3. The word _____ comes from the Latin word linearis, which means created by lines.
   a. Thing
   b. Linear3
   c. Undefined
   d. Undefined

4. In mathematics, a _____ is a rectangular table of numbers or, more generally, a table consisting of abstract quantities that can be added and multiplied.
   a. Matrix4
   b. Thing
   c. Undefined
   d. Undefined

5. In plane geometry, a _____ is a polygon with four equal sides, four right angles, and parallel opposite sides. In algebra, the _____ of a number is that number multiplied by itself.
   a. Square5
   b. Thing
   c. Undefined
   d. Undefined

6. In mathematics, a _____ of a number x is a number r such that r^2 = x, or in words, a number r whose square (the result of multiplying the number by itself) is x.

Chapter 9. Systems of Linear Equations in Three Variables

a. Square root6
b. Thing
c. Undefined
d. Undefined

7. In set theory and other branches of mathematics, the _____ of a collection of sets is the set that contains everything that belongs to any of the sets, but nothing else.
   a. Thing
   b. Union7
   c. Undefined
   d. Undefined

8. In mathematics, a _____ of a complex-valued function f is a member x of the domain of f such that f(x) vanishes at x, that is, x : f (x) = 0.
   a. Thing
   b. Root8
   c. Undefined
   d. Undefined

9. In linear algebra, _____ elimination is a version of Gaussian elimination that puts zeros both above and below each pivot element as it goes from the top row of the given matrix to the bottom. In other words, _____ elimination brings a matrix to reduced row echelon form, whereas Gaussian elimination takes it only as far as row echelon form.
   a. Gauss-Jordan9
   b. Thing
   c. Undefined
   d. Undefined

10. Mathematical _____ is used in mathematics, and throughout the physical sciences, engineering, and economics. The complexity of such _____ ranges from relatively simple symbolic representations, such as numbers 1 and 2; function symbols sin and +, to conceptual symbols, such as lim and dy/dx; to equations and variables.
    a. Notation10
    b. Thing
    c. Undefined
    d. Undefined

11. The mathematical concept of a _____ expresses the intuitive idea of deterministic dependence between two quantities, one of which is viewed as primary and the other as secondary. A _____ then is a way to associate a unique output for each input of a specified type, for example, a real number or an element of a given set.
   a. Function11
   b. Thing
   c. Undefined
   d. Undefined

Chapter 10. More Equations and Inequalities

1. In mathematics, the _____ of two sets A and B is the set that contains all elements of A that also belong to B (or equivalently, all elements of B that also belong to A), but no other elements.
   a. Intersection1
   b. Thing
   c. Undefined
   d. Undefined

2. In set theory and other branches of mathematics, the _____ of a collection of sets is the set that contains everything that belongs to any of the sets, but nothing else.
   a. Union2
   b. Thing
   c. Undefined
   d. Undefined

3. Mathematical _____ is used in mathematics, and throughout the physical sciences, engineering, and economics. The complexity of such _____ ranges from relatively simple symbolic representations, such as numbers 1 and 2; function symbols sin and +, to conceptual symbols, such as lim and dy/dx; to equations and variables.
   a. Thing
   b. Notation3
   c. Undefined
   d. Undefined

4. In mathematics, a _____ is an expression that is constructed from one or more variables and constants, using only the operations of addition, subtraction, multiplication, and constant positive whole number exponents. is a _____. Note in particular that division by an expression containing a variable is not in general allowed in polynomials.
   a. Thing
   b. Polynomial4
   c. Undefined
   d. Undefined

5. In mathematics, a _____ is a polynomial equation of the second degree. The general form is $ax^2 + bx + c = 0$.
   a. Quadratic equation5
   b. Thing
   c. Undefined
   d. Undefined

Chapter 10. More Equations and Inequalities

6. An _____ is a mathematical statement, in symbols, that two things are the same or equivalent. Equations are written with an equal sign, as in 2 + 3 = 5.
   a. Equation6
   b. Thing
   c. Undefined
   d. Undefined

7. A _____ is a symbolic representation denoting a quantity or expression. It often represents an "unknown" quantity that has the potential to change.
   a. Variable7
   b. Thing
   c. Undefined
   d. Undefined

8. The word _____ comes from the Latin word linearis, which means created by lines.
   a. Linear8
   b. Thing
   c. Undefined
   d. Undefined

Chapter 11. Radicals and Complex Numbers

1. In mathematics, a _____ may be described informally as a number that can be given by an infinite decimal representation.
   a. Real number1
   b. Thing
   c. Undefined
   d. Undefined

2. In mathematics, a _____ of a complex-valued function f is a member x of the domain of f such that f(x) vanishes at x, that is, x : f (x) = 0.
   a. Root2
   b. Thing
   c. Undefined
   d. Undefined

3. In plane geometry, a _____ is a polygon with four equal sides, four right angles, and parallel opposite sides. In algebra, the _____ of a number is that number multiplied by itself.
   a. Square3
   b. Thing
   c. Undefined
   d. Undefined

4. In mathematics, a _____ of a number x is a number r such that r^2 = x, or in words, a number r whose square (the result of multiplying the number by itself) is x.
   a. Square root4
   b. Thing
   c. Undefined
   d. Undefined

5. A _____ of a number is a number a such that a^3 = x.
   a. Cube root5
   b. Thing
   c. Undefined
   d. Undefined

6. _____ usually occurs when an exact form or an exact numerical number is unknown.

Chapter 11. Radicals and Complex Numbers 33

a. Thing
b. Approximation6
c. Undefined
d. Undefined

7. In mathematics, a _____ of a k-place relation $L \subseteq X_1 \times ... \times X_k$ is one of the sets X_j, $1 \le j \le k$. In the special case where k = 2 and $L \subseteq X_1 \times X_2$ is a function $L : X_1 \to X_2$, it is conventional to refer to X_1 as the _____ of the function and to refer to X_2 as the codomain of the function.
    a. Thing
    b. Domain7
    c. Undefined
    d. Undefined

8. The mathematical concept of a _____ expresses the intuitive idea of deterministic dependence between two quantities, one of which is viewed as primary and the other as secondary. A _____ then is a way to associate a unique output for each input of a specified type, for example, a real number or an element of a given set.
    a. Function8
    b. Thing
    c. Undefined
    d. Undefined

9. In mathematics, a _____ is a statement that can be proved on the basis of explicitly stated or previously agreed assumptions.
    a. Theorem9
    b. Thing
    c. Undefined
    d. Undefined

10. A _____ is a symbolic representation denoting a quantity or expression. It often represents an "unknown" quantity that has the potential to change.
    a. Thing
    b. Variable10
    c. Undefined
    d. Undefined

11. _____ is a mathematical operation, written a^n, involving two numbers, the base a and the exponent n.

Chapter 11. Radicals and Complex Numbers

a. Thing
b. Exponentiating11
c. Undefined
d. Undefined

12. Mathematical _____ is used in mathematics, and throughout the physical sciences, engineering, and economics. The complexity of such _____ ranges from relatively simple symbolic representations, such as numbers 1 and 2; function symbols sin and +, to conceptual symbols, such as lim and dy/dx; to equations and variables.
   a. Notation12
   b. Thing
   c. Undefined
   d. Undefined

13. In mathematics, the _____ of two sets A and B is the set that contains all elements of A that also belong to B (or equivalently, all elements of B that also belong to A), but no other elements.
   a. Intersection13
   b. Thing
   c. Undefined
   d. Undefined

14. A _____ is a special kind of ratio, indicating a relationship between two measurements with different units, such as miles to gallons or cents to pounds.
   a. Thing
   b. Rate14
   c. Undefined
   d. Undefined

15. In philosophy, mathematics, and logic, a _____ is an attribute of an object; thus a red object is said to have the _____ of redness.
   a. Property15
   b. Thing
   c. Undefined
   d. Undefined

16. _____ is the mathematical operation of combining or adding two numbers to obtain an equal simple amount or total.

Chapter 11. Radicals and Complex Numbers

  a. Addition16
  b. Thing
  c. Undefined
  d. Undefined

17. An _____ is a mathematical statement, in symbols, that two things are the same or equivalent. Equations are written with an equal sign, as in 2 + 3 = 5.
  a. Equation17
  b. Thing
  c. Undefined
  d. Undefined

18. In mathematics, a _____ is a number in the form of a + bi where a and b are real numbers, and i is the imaginary unit, with the property $i^2 = -1$. The real number a is called the real part of the _____, and the real number b is the imaginary part.
  a. Thing
  b. Complex number18
  c. Undefined
  d. Undefined

19. _____ is a notation for writing numbers that is often used by scientists and mathematicians to make it easier to write large and small numbers.
  a. Scientific notation19
  b. Thing
  c. Undefined
  d. Undefined

Chapter 12. Quadratic Equations and Functions

1. In mathematics, a _____ is a polynomial equation of the second degree. The general form is $ax^2 + bx + c = 0$.
   a. Quadratic equation1
   b. Thing
   c. Undefined
   d. Undefined

2. In mathematics, a _____ of a complex-valued function f is a member x of the domain of f such that f(x) vanishes at x, that is, $x : f(x) = 0$.
   a. Root2
   b. Thing
   c. Undefined
   d. Undefined

3. In plane geometry, a _____ is a polygon with four equal sides, four right angles, and parallel opposite sides. In algebra, the _____ of a number is that number multiplied by itself.
   a. Square3
   b. Thing
   c. Undefined
   d. Undefined

4. In mathematics, a _____ of a number x is a number r such that $r^2 = x$, or in words, a number r whose square (the result of multiplying the number by itself) is x.
   a. Thing
   b. Square root4
   c. Undefined
   d. Undefined

5. The word _____ comes from the Latin word linearis, which means created by lines.
   a. Thing
   b. Linear5
   c. Undefined
   d. Undefined

6. An _____ is a mathematical statement, in symbols, that two things are the same or equivalent. Equations are written with an equal sign, as in $2 + 3 = 5$.

Chapter 12. Quadratic Equations and Functions

a. Equation6
b. Thing
c. Undefined
d. Undefined

7. A quadratic equation with real solutions, called roots, which may be real or complex, is given by the _____: $x = \frac{-b \pm \sqrt{b^2 - 4ac}}{2a}$.
   a. Quadratic formula7
   b. Thing
   c. Undefined
   d. Undefined

8. The _____ governs the differentiation of products of differentiable functions.
   a. Thing
   b. Product rule8
   c. Undefined
   d. Undefined

9. The mathematical concept of a _____ expresses the intuitive idea of deterministic dependence between two quantities, one of which is viewed as primary and the other as secondary. A _____ then is a way to associate a unique output for each input of a specified type, for example, a real number or an element of a given set.
   a. Thing
   b. Function9
   c. Undefined
   d. Undefined

10. A _____ is a symbolic representation denoting a quantity or expression. It often represents an "unknown" quantity that has the potential to change.
    a. Variable10
    b. Thing
    c. Undefined
    d. Undefined

11. In philosophy, mathematics, and logic, a _____ is an attribute of an object; thus a red object is said to have the _____ of redness.

a. Thing
b. Property11
c. Undefined
d. Undefined

12. In astronomy, geography, geometry and related sciences and contexts, a plane is said to be _____ at a given point if it is locally perpendicular to the gradient of the gravity field, i.e., with the direction of the gravitational force at that point.
    a. Horizontal12
    b. Thing
    c. Undefined
    d. Undefined

13. In mathematics, the _____ is a conic section generated by the intersection of a right circular conical surface and a plane parallel to a generating straight line of that surface. It can also be defined as locus of points in a plane which are equidistant from a given point.
    a. Thing
    b. Parabola13
    c. Undefined
    d. Undefined

14. In geometry, a _____ is a special kind of point, usually a corner of a polygon, polyhedron, or higher dimensional polytope. In the geometry of curves a _____ is a point of where the first derivative of curvature is zero. In graph theory, a _____ is the fundamental unit out of which graphs are formed
    a. Vertex14
    b. Thing
    c. Undefined
    d. Undefined

Chapter 13. Exponential and Logarithmic Functions

1. An _____ is a function which does the reverse of a given function.
   a. Inverse function1
   b. Thing
   c. Undefined
   d. Undefined

2. The word _____ comes from the Latin word linearis, which means created by lines.
   a. Linear2
   b. Thing
   c. Undefined
   d. Undefined

3. _____ is the mathematical operation of combining or adding two numbers to obtain an equal simple amount or total.
   a. Addition3
   b. Thing
   c. Undefined
   d. Undefined

4. An _____ is a mathematical statement, in symbols, that two things are the same or equivalent. Equations are written with an equal sign, as in 2 + 3 = 5.
   a. Equation4
   b. Thing
   c. Undefined
   d. Undefined

5. The mathematical concept of a _____ expresses the intuitive idea of deterministic dependence between two quantities, one of which is viewed as primary and the other as secondary. A _____ then is a way to associate a unique output for each input of a specified type, for example, a real number or an element of a given set.
   a. Thing
   b. Function5
   c. Undefined
   d. Undefined

6. In mathematics, a _____ is a polynomial equation of the second degree. The general form is $ax^2 + bx + c = 0$.

Chapter 13. Exponential and Logarithmic Functions

   a. Thing
   b. Quadratic equation6
   c. Undefined
   d. Undefined

7. Mathematical _____ is used in mathematics, and throughout the physical sciences, engineering, and economics. The complexity of such _____ ranges from relatively simple symbolic representations, such as numbers 1 and 2; function symbols sin and +, to conceptual symbols, such as lim and dy/dx; to equations and variables.
   a. Thing
   b. Notation7
   c. Undefined
   d. Undefined

8. In mathematics, a _____ of a k-place relation $L \subseteq X_1 \times \ldots \times X_k$ is one of the sets X_j, $1 \leq j \leq k$. In the special case where k = 2 and $L \subseteq X_1 \times X_2$ is a function $L : X_1 \to X_2$, it is conventional to refer to X_1 as the _____ of the function and to refer to X_2 as the codomain of the function.
   a. Thing
   b. Domain8
   c. Undefined
   d. Undefined

9. In mathematics, the _____ of a function is the set of all "output" values produced by that function. Given a function $f : A \to B$, the _____ of f, is defined to be the set $\{x \in B : x = f(a) \text{ for some } a \in A\}$.
   a. Range9
   b. Thing
   c. Undefined
   d. Undefined

10. In astronomy, geography, geometry and related sciences and contexts, a plane is said to be _____ at a given point if it is locally perpendicular to the gradient of the gravity field, i.e., with the direction of the gravitational force at that point.
   a. Thing
   b. Horizontal10
   c. Undefined
   d. Undefined

Chapter 13. Exponential and Logarithmic Functions

11. _____ is one of the most important functions in mathematics. A function commonly used to study growth and decay
   a. Thing
   b. Exponential function11
   c. Undefined
   d. Undefined

12. _____ usually occurs when an exact form or an exact numerical number is unknown.
   a. Approximation12
   b. Thing
   c. Undefined
   d. Undefined

13. _____ is an inexact representation of something that is still close enough to be useful. Although approximation is most often applied to numbers, it is also frequently applied to such things as mathematical functions, shapes, and physical laws.
   a. Thing
   b. Approximating13
   c. Undefined
   d. Undefined

14. In mathematics, a _____ is the end result of a division problem. It can also be expressed as the number of times the divisor divides into the dividend.
   a. Thing
   b. Quotient14
   c. Undefined
   d. Undefined

15. In mathematics, a _____ of a number x is the exponent y of the power by such that $x = b^y$. The value used for the base b must be neither 0 nor 1, nor a root of 1 in the case of the extension to complex numbers, and is typically 10, e, or 2.
   a. Logarithm15
   b. Thing
   c. Undefined
   d. Undefined

16. In philosophy, mathematics, and logic, a _____ is an attribute of an object; thus a red object is said to have the _____ of redness.
   a. Thing
   b. Property16
   c. Undefined
   d. Undefined

Chapter 14. Conic Sections and Nonlinear Systems

1. An _____ is a mathematical statement, in symbols, that two things are the same or equivalent. Equations are written with an equal sign, as in 2 + 3 = 5.
   a. Equation1
   b. Thing
   c. Undefined
   d. Undefined

2. In classical geometry, a _____ of a circle or sphere is any line segment from its center to its boundary. By extension, the _____ of a circle or sphere is the length of any such segment. The _____ is half the diameter. In science and engineering the term _____ of curvature is commonly used as a synonym for _____.
   a. Radius2
   b. Thing
   c. Undefined
   d. Undefined

3. _____ is a notation for writing numbers that is often used by scientists and mathematicians to make it easier to write large and small numbers.
   a. Thing
   b. Scientific notation3
   c. Undefined
   d. Undefined

4. In Euclidean geometry, a _____ is the set of all points in a plane at a fixed distance, called the radius, from a given point, the center.
   a. Thing
   b. Circle4
   c. Undefined
   d. Undefined

5. In mathematics, the _____ is a conic section generated by the intersection of a right circular conical surface and a plane parallel to a generating straight line of that surface. It can also be defined as locus of points in a plane which are equidistant from a given point.
   a. Parabola5
   b. Thing
   c. Undefined
   d. Undefined

6. In geometry, a _____ is a special kind of point, usually a corner of a polygon, polyhedron, or higher dimensional polytope. In the geometry of curves a _____ is a point of where the first derivative of curvature is zero. In graph theory, a _____ is the fundamental unit out of which graphs are formed
   a. Vertex6
   b. Thing
   c. Undefined
   d. Undefined

7. The word _____ comes from the Latin word linearis, which means created by lines.
   a. Thing
   b. Linear7
   c. Undefined
   d. Undefined

8. In astronomy, geography, geometry and related sciences and contexts, a plane is said to be _____ at a given point if it is locally perpendicular to the gradient of the gravity field, i.e., with the direction of the gravitational force at that point.
   a. Thing
   b. Horizontal8
   c. Undefined
   d. Undefined

9. In plane geometry, a _____ is a polygon with four equal sides, four right angles, and parallel opposite sides. In algebra, the _____ of a number is that number multiplied by itself.
   a. Thing
   b. Square9
   c. Undefined
   d. Undefined

10. _____ is the mathematical operation of combining or adding two numbers to obtain an equal simple amount or total.
    a. Addition10
    b. Thing
    c. Undefined
    d. Undefined

Chapter 14. Conic Sections and Nonlinear Systems

11. A _____ is a symbolic representation denoting a quantity or expression. It often represents an "unknown" quantity that has the potential to change.
    a. Thing
    b. Variable11
    c. Undefined
    d. Undefined

12. In geometry, the _____ are a pair of special points used in describing conic sections. The four types of conic sections are the circle, parabola, ellipse, and hyperbola.
    a. Foci12
    b. Thing
    c. Undefined
    d. Undefined

ANSWER KEY

Chapter 1
1. b 2. b 3. a 4. b 5. b 6. a 7. a 8. b 9. a 10. a
11. a 12. b 13. a 14. b 15. b 16. a 17. b 18. a 19. a 20. b
21. b 22. b 23. a 24. a 25. b 26. b 27. b 28. a 29. b 30. b
31. a 32. b 33. a 34. a 35. b

Chapter 2
1. b 2. a 3. a 4. a 5. a 6. b 7. b 8. b 9. a 10. a
11. a 12. a 13. a 14. a 15. b

Chapter 3
1. b 2. a 3. b 4. a 5. b 6. b 7. b 8. a 9. a 10. a
11. a

Chapter 4
1. a 2. b 3. a 4. b

Chapter 5
1. b 2. a 3. b 4. a 5. b 6. a 7. a 8. b 9. b 10. a
11. b 12. b

Chapter 6
1. a 2. b 3. a 4. a 5. a 6. a 7. a 8. b 9. b 10. a
11. b 12. a 13. b 14. a 15. b 16. b

Chapter 7
1. a 2. b 3. a 4. a 5. b 6. b 7. a 8. a 9. b 10. a

Chapter 8
1. b 2. a 3. b 4. b 5. b 6. b 7. b 8. b 9. b 10. a
11. b 12. b

Chapter 9
1. a 2. a 3. b 4. a 5. a 6. a 7. b 8. b 9. a 10. a
11. a

Chapter 10
1. a 2. a 3. b 4. b 5. a 6. a 7. a 8. a

Chapter 11
1. a 2. a 3. a 4. a 5. a 6. b 7. b 8. a 9. a 10. b
11. b 12. a 13. a 14. b 15. a 16. a 17. a 18. b 19. a

Chapter 12
1. a 2. a 3. a 4. b 5. b 6. a 7. a 8. b 9. b 10. a
11. b 12. a 13. b 14. a

ANSWER KEY

Chapter 13
1. a   2. a   3. a   4. a   5. b   6. b   7. b   8. b   9. a   10. b
11. b   12. a   13. b   14. b   15. a   16. b

Chapter 14
1. a   2. a   3. b   4. b   5. a   6. a   7. b   8. b   9. b   10. a
11. b   12. a